Joy to the World

Christmas Carols for Organ

arranged by **Carolyn Hamlin**

table of contents

for my daughters and their husbands: Tammy and David Day, Tracy and Rick Redmon, and Terry and Keith Batson

Noel, Noel, Noel, Tidings Now We Bring

A medley, including:
Masters in This Hall
God Rest Ye Merry, Gentlemen
On Christmas Night All Christians Sing
Once in Royal David's City

Arr. by Carolyn Hamlin (ASCAP)

REGISTRATIONS:
Due to the length of the recommended registrations (two sets: traditional and MIDI), they are listed separately on pages 8-9.

With great joy ♩ = 92

"On Christmas Night All Christians Sing" (Traditional English Carol)

Sw.
Gt.
Gt.
Gen. 1
rit.

"Once in Royal David's City" (Music by Henry John Gauntlett)

Gen. 5
54
Gt.
Sw.
58
With renewed vigor
62
Gen. 6
Gt.
Ch.
Gt.
65

68
Gt.
71
74
ten.
slight rit.
Ch.
Much slower
77
Gen. 7
Gt.

Traditional Registration

GENERAL 1: Sw: Viola 8', Rohr Bourdon 8', Principal 4', Piccolo 2', Mixture IV, Bassoon 16', Trumpet 8', Clarion 4'
Gt: Diapason 8', Octave 4', Fifteenth 2', Mixture IV, Scharf III, Sw. to Gt. 8', Ch. to Gt. 8'
Ch: Gedeckt 8', Principal 4', Octave 2', Quintflöte 1-1/3', Zimbel III, Sw. to Ch. 8'
Ped: Bourdon 16', Violone 16', Octave 8', Choralbass 4', Mixture IV, Bombarde 16', Bassoon 16', Gt. to Ped. 8', Sw. to Ped. 8', Ch. to Ped. 8'

GENERAL 2: Sw: Trumpet 8'
Gt: Diapason 8', Octave 4'
Ch: Gedeckt 8', Koppelflöte 4', Quintflöte 1-1/3'
Ped: Violone 16', Lieblich Gedeckt 16', Gedeckt 8'

GENERAL 3: Sw: Oboe 8'
Gt: Harmonic Flute 8'
Gt. Divisional I: Harmonic Flute 8', Spitzflöte 4'
Ch: Krummhorn 8'
Ped: Lieblich Gedeckt 16', Gedeckt 8'

GENERAL 4: Sw: Viola 8', Viola Celeste 8', Flute Celeste II 8', Vox Humana 8', Tremulant
Gt: Gamba 8', Tremulant, Sw. to Gt. 16', 8', 4', Ch. to Gt. 8'
Ch: Erzähler 16', 8', Erzähler Celeste 8', Erzähler Celeste II 4', Tremulant
Ped: Bourdon 32', 16', Violone 16', Sw. to Ped. 8', Ch. to Ped. 8'

GENERAL 5: Sw: Flute 4', Trumpet 8', Tremulant
Gt: Gamba 8', Tremulant, Ch. to Gt. 8'
Ch: Erzähler 16', 8', Erzähler Celeste 8', Erzähler Celeste II 4', Tremulant
Ped: Bourdon 32', Violone 16', Ch. to Ped. 8'

GENERAL 6: Sw: Viola 8', Rohr Bourdon 8', Principal 4', Piccolo 2', Mixture IV, Bassoon 16', Trumpet 8', Clarion 4'
Gt: Diapason 8', Octave 4', Fifteenth 2', Mixture IV, Scharf III, Sw. to Gt. 8'
Ch: Festival Trumpet 8', Choir Unenclosed
Ped: Bourdon 32', 16', Diapason 16', Violone 16', Octave 8', Choralbass 4', Gt. to Ped. 8', Sw. to Ped. 8'

GENERAL 7: Sw: Viola 8', Rohr Bourdon 8', Principal 4', Piccolo 2', Mixture IV, Bassoon 16', Trumpet 8', Clarion 4'
Gt: Diapason 8', Octave 4', Fifteenth 2', Mixture IV, Scharf III, Double Trumpet 16', Tromba 8', Sw. to Gt. 8', Ch. to Gt. 8'
Ch: Gedeckt 8', Principal 4', Octave 2', Zimbel III
Ped: Bourdon 32', 16', Diapason 16', Violone 16', Octave 8', Choralbass 4', Contre Bombarde 32', Bombarde 16', Trompette 8', Gt. to Ped. 8', Sw. to Ped. 8', Ch. to Ped. 8'

MIDI Registration

GENERAL 1: Sw: (no stops)
Gt: Tromba 8', MIDI Bugle
Ch: (no stops)
Ped: Bombarde 16', MIDI Bugle

GENERAL 2: Sw: MIDI Bugle
Gt: MIDI Brass Ensemble*
Ch: MIDI Oboe
Ped: Bourdon 16', Gedeckt 8'

GENERAL 3: Sw: Viola 8', Viola Celeste 8', Tremulant, Swell Unison Off, MIDI Oboe*
Gt: Gamba 8, Tremulant, Sw. to Gt. 8', MIDI Strings*
Gt. Divisional I: Gamba 8', Spitzflöte 4', Tremulant, Sw. to Gt. 8', 4', MIDI Octave Violin*
Ch: MIDI Clarinet*
Ped: Violone 16', Sw. to Ped. 8', MIDI Strings*

GENERAL 4: Sw: Viola 8', Viola Celeste 8', Flute Celeste II 8', Vox Humana 8', Tremulant, MIDI Strings*
Gt: Gamba 8', Tremulant, Sw. to Gt. 16', 8'
Ch: Erzähler 16', 8', Erzähler Celeste 8', Erzähler Celeste II 4', Tremulant
Ped: Bourdon 32', 16', Violone 16', Sw. to Ped. 8', Ch. to Ped. 8', MIDI Strings*

GENERAL 5: Sw: MIDI Oboe*
Gt: Gamba 8', Harmonic Flute 8', Tremulant, Ch. to Gt. 8', MIDI Strings*
Ch: Erzähler 16', 8', Erzähler Celeste 8', Erzähler Celeste II 4', Tremulant
Ped: Bourdon 32', 16', Violone 16', Sw. to Ped. 8', Ch. to Ped. 8', MIDI Strings*

GENERAL 6: Sw: Viola 8', Rohr Bourdon 8', Principal 4', Piccolo 2', Mixture IV, Bassoon 16', Trumpet 8', Clarion 4'
Gt: Diapason 8', Octave 4', Fifteenth 2', Mixture IV, Scharf III, Sw. to Gt. 8'
Ch: Festival Trumpet 8', MIDI Bugle, Choir Unenclosed
Ped: Bourdon 32', 16', Diapason 16', Violone 16', Octave 8', Choralbass 4', Gt. to Ped. 8', Sw. to Ped. 8'

GENERAL 7: Sw: Viola 8', Rohr Bourdon 8', Principal 4', Piccolo 2', Mixture IV, Bassoon 16', Trumpet 8', Clarion 4'
Gt: Diapason 8', Octave 4', Fifteenth 2', Mixture IV, Scharf III, Double Trumpet 16', Tromba 8', Sw. to Gt. 8', Ch. to Gt. 8', MIDI Bugle
Ch: Gedeckt 8', Principal 4', Octave 2', Zimbel III
Ped: Bourdon 32', 16', Diapason 16', Violone 16', Octave 8', Choralbass 4', Contre Bombarde 32', Bombarde 16', Trompette 8', Gt. to Ped. 8', Sw. to Ped. 8', Ch. to Ped. 8', MIDI Bugle

*Tremulant

for Frances Young Austin

O Holy Night

REGISTRATIONS:
Due to their extensive detail, both traditional and MIDI registrations are listed separately on page 17.

CANTIQUE DE NOEL
Adolphe C. Adams
Arr. by Carolyn Hamlin (ASCAP)

In a singing style ♩. = 60

10
Gt.
13
16
Sw. 1
Ch.
19
Gt.

22
Gt.
25
Gen. 2
Gt.
Ch.
28
31

34
37
Gt.
40
poco rit.
43
Gen. 3
Gt.
a tempo

46
49
Gen. 4
Sw.
53
Gt.
56
Gt.

59
poco rit.
62
Gen. 5
Gt.
a tempo
65
68

71
75
Gen. 6
Much slower to end
Sw.
rit.
Ch.
79
Gt.
82
Gen. 7
Sw.
slowing to end
Ch.
Ped. 1

Traditional Registration

General 1: Sw. Viola 8', Viola Cel. 8', Fl. Cel. II 8', Fl. 4', Vox Humana 8', Trem.
Sw. Divisional 1: Viola 8', Viola Cel. 8', Fl. Cel. II 8', Fl. 4', Vox Humana 8', Trem., Sw. to Sw. 16', Swell Unison Off
Gt. Harmonic Fl. 8', Spitzflöte 4', Trem., Ch. to Gt. 8'
Ch Ged. 8', Erzähler 8', Erzähler Cel. 8', Trem., Celesta
Ped. Violone 16', Lieb. Ged. 16', Ch. to Ped. 8'

General 2: Sw Viola 8', Viola Cel. 8', Fl. Cel. II 8', Vox Humana 8', Trem.
Gt. Harmonic Fl. 8', Spitzflöte 4', Trem., Sw. to Gt. 8', 4'
Ch Ged. 8', Erzähler 8', Erzähler Cel. 8', Koppelflöte 4', Trem.
Ped. Violone 16', Lieb. Ged. 8', Ged. 8'

General 3: Sw. Viola 8', Rohr Bourdon 8', Principal 4', Piccolo 2'
Gt. Diap. 8', Harm. Fl. 8', Oct. 4', Sw. to Gt. 8', Ch. to Gt. 8'
Ch Ged. 8', Principal 4'
Ped. Bourdon 16', Violone 16', Ged. 8', Sw. to Ped. 8', Ch. to Ped. 8'

General 4: Sw. Trumpet 8', Sw. to Sw. 16'
Gt. Diap. 8', Harm. Fl. 8', Oct. 4', Ch. to Gt. 8'
Ch Ged. 8', Principal 4'
Ped. Bourdon 16', Violone 16', Ged. 8', Ch. to Ped. 8'

General 5: Sw. Lieb. Bourdon 16', Viola 8', Rohr Bourdon 8', Prin. 4', Piccolo 2', Mixture IV, Bassoon 16', Trumpet 8', Clarion 4'
Gt. Violone 16', Diap. 8', Harm. Fl. 8', Oct. 4', Twelfth 2-2/3', Fifteenth 2', Sw. to Gt. 8', Ch. to Gt. 8'
Ch. Ged. 8', Principal 4', Oct. 2'
Ped. Bourdon 32', 16', Diap. 16', Violone 16', Oct. 8', Gt. to Ped. 8, Sw. to Ped. 8, Ch. to Ped. 8'

General 6: Sw. Oboe 8', Trem.
Gt. Gamba 8', Spitzflöte 4', Trem.
Ch. Erzähler 8', Erzähler Cel. 8'
Ped. Lieb. Ged. 16', Ch. to Ped. 8'

General 7: Sw. Flute 4', Trem.
Gt. (no stops)
Ch. Erzähler 8', Erzähler Cel. 8'
Ped. Lieb. Ged. 16', Ch. to Ped. 8'
Ped. Divisional 1: Bourdon 32', Lieb. Ged. 16', Ch. to Ped. 8'

MIDI Registration (* = trem.)

General 1: Sw. Viola 8', Viola Cel. 8', Fl. Cel. II 8', Fl. 4', Vox Humana 8', Trem., Swell Unison Off, MIDI Solo Violin*
Sw. Divisional 1: Viola 8', Viola Cel. 8', Fl. Cel. II 8', Fl. 4', Vox Humana 8', Trem., Swell Unison Off, MIDI Oboe*
Gt. Gamba 8', Trem., Sw. to Gt. 8', Ch. to Gt. 8', MIDI Strings*
Ch. Erzähler 8', Erzähler Cel. 8', MIDI Orchestral Harp
Ped. Violone 16', Lieb. Ged. 16', Ch. to Ped. 8'

General 2: Sw. (no stops)
Gt. Harmonic Fl. 8', MIDI French Horn
Ch. Erzähler 8', Erzähler Cel. 8', MIDI Orchestral Harp
Ped. Lieb. Ged. 8', Ch. to Ped. 8'

General 3: Sw. Viola 8', Viola Cel. 8', Rohr Bourdon 8', Fl. Cel. II 8', Trem.
Gt. Diap. 8', Gamba 8', Trem., Sw. to Gt. 8', 4', Ch. to Gt. 8', MIDI Strings*
Ch. Ged. 8', Erzähler 8', Erzähler Cel. 8', Principal 4', Trem.
Ped. Bourdon 16', Violone 16', Sw. to Ped. 8', Ch. to Ped. 8'

General 4: Sw. MIDI Cast Bells
Gt Diap. 8', Harm. Fl. 8', Oct. 4', Ch. to Gt. 8'
Ch. Ged. 8', Principal 4'
Ped. Bourdon 16', Ch. to Ped. 8'

General 5: Sw. Lieb. Bourdon 16', Viola 8', Rohr Bourdon 8', Prin. 4', Piccolo 2', Bassoon 16', Trumpet 8'
Gt Violone 16', Diap. 8', Harm. Fl. 8', Oct. 4', Twelfth 2-2/3', Fifteenth 2', Sw. to Gt. 8', Ch. to Gt. 8', MIDI Strings*
Ch. Ged. 8', Principal 4', Oct. 2'
Ped. Bourdon 32', 16', Diap. 16', Violone 16', Oct. 8', Gt. to Ped. 8, Sw. to Ped. 8, Ch. to Ped. 8', MIDI Strings *

General 6: Sw. MIDI Clarinet*
Gt. MIDI Violin*
Ch. Erzähler 8', Erzähler Cel. 8', MIDI Orchestral Harp
Ped. Lieb. Ged. 16', Ch. to Ped. 8'

General 7: Sw. MIDI Piccolo
Gt. (no stops)
Ch. Erzähler 8', Erzähler Cel. 8', MIDI Orchestral Harp
Ped. Lieb. Ged. 16', Ch. to Ped. 8'
Ped. Divisional 1: Bourdon 32', Lieb. Ged. 16', Ch. to Ped. 8'

for Dave Kirk

Joy to the World! The Lord Is Come

with **Hallelujah Chorus**

Due to the complexity of registrations used, they are included separately on page 24.

ANTIOCH
G. F. Handel; adapted by Lowell Mason
Arr. by Carolyn Hamlin
(ASCAP)

With joy and grandeur ♩ = 86

10
13
16
20

24
Gt.
Ch.
27
30
33

36
Gen. 2
Gt.
39
42
Ch.
Gt.
45
poco rit.

More majestic
48
Ch.
51
Gt.
54
57

60
63
Gen. 3
poco rit.
66
69
molto rit.
Ped. 1

Traditional Registration

Gen. 1: Sw. Viola 8', Gedeckt 8', Principal 4', Piccolo 2', Mixture IV
Gt. Diapason 8', Bourdon 8', Octave 4', Spitzflöte 4', Sw. to Gt. 8'
Ch. Festival Trumpet 8'
Ped. Bourdon 16', Violone 16', Octave 8', Choralbass 4', Bassoon 16', Gt. to Ped. 8', Sw. to Ped. 8'

Gen. 2: Sw. Viola 8', Gedeckt 8', Principal 4', Piccolo 2', Mixture IV, Bassoon 16', Trompette 8', Clarion 4'
Gt. Diap. 8', Harm. Flute 8', Octave 4', Fifteenth 2', Mixture IV, Double Tpt. 16', Tpt. 8', Sw. to Gt. 8'
Ch. Festival Trumpet 8'
Ped. Bourdon 32', 16', Diap. 16', Violone 16', Oct. 8', Flute 8', Choralbass 4', Bombarde 16', Trompette 8', Gt. to Ped. 8', Sw. to Ped. 8'

Gen. 3: Sw. Viola 8', Gedeckt 8', Principal 4', Piccolo 2', Mixture IV, Bassoon 16', Trompette 8', Clarion 4'
Gt. Diap. 8', Harm. Fl. 8', Oct. 4', Fifteenth 2', Mix. IV, Double Tpt. 16', Tpt. 8', Sw. to Gt. 8', Ch. to Gt. 8'
Ch. Gedeckt 8', Principal 4', Octave 2', Zimbel III, Sw. to Ch. 8'
Ped. Bourdon 32', 16', Diap. 16', Violone 16', Oct. 8', Flute 8', Choralbass 4', Bombarde 16', Trompette 8', Clarion 4', Gt. to Ped. 8', Sw. to Ped. 8', Ch. to Ped. 8'

Ped. Divisional 1: Bourdon 32', 16', Diap. 16', Violone 16', Oct. 8', Flute 8', Choralbass 4', Mixture IV, Contre Bombarde 32', Bombarde 16', Trompette 8', Clarion 4', Gt. to Ped. 8', Sw. to Ped. 8', Ch. to Ped. 8'

MIDI Registration

Gen. 1: Sw. Viola 8', Gedeckt 8', Principal 4', Piccolo 2', Mixture IV
Gt. Diapason 8', Bourdon 8', Octave 4', Spitzflöte 4', Sw. to Gt. 8', MIDI Harpsichord
Ch. MIDI Bugle
Ped. Bourdon 16', Violone 16', Octave 8', Choralbass 4', Bassoon 16', Gt. to Ped. 8', Sw. to Ped. 8', MIDI harpsichord

Gen. 2: Sw. Viola 8', Gedeckt 8', Principal 4', Piccolo 2', Mixture IV, Bassoon 16', Trompette 8', Clarion 4'
Gt. Diap. 8', Harm. Flute 8', Octave 4', Fifteenth 2', Mixture IV, Double Tpt. 16', Tpt. 8', Sw. to Gt. 8', MIDI Harpsichord
Ch. MIDI Bugle
Ped. Bourdon 32', 16', Diap. 16', Violone 16', Oct. 8', Flute 8', Choralbass 4', Bombarde 16', Trompette 8', Gt. to Ped. 8', Sw. to Ped. 8', MIDI Harpsichord

Gen. 3: Sw. Viola 8', Gedeckt 8', Principal 4', Piccolo 2', Mixture IV, Bassoon 16', Trompette 8', Clarion 4'
Gt. Diap. 8', Harm. Fl. 8', Oct. 4', Fifteenth 2', Mix. IV, Double Tpt. 16', Tpt. 8', Sw. to Gt. 8', Ch. to Gt. 8'
Ch. Gedeckt 8', Principal 4', Octave 2', Zimbel III, Sw. to Ch. 8'
Ped. Bourdon 32', 16', Diap. 16', Violone 16', Oct. 8', Flute 8', Choralbass 4', Bombarde 16', Trompette 8', Clarion 4', Gt. to Ped. 8', Sw. to Ped. 8', Ch. to Ped. 8', MIDI Timpani

Ped. Divisional 1: Bourdon 32', 16', Diap. 16', Violone 16', Oct. 8', Flute 8', Choralbass 4', Mixture IV, Contre Bombarde 32', Bombarde 16', Trompette 8', Clarion 4', Gt. to Ped. 8', Sw. to Ped. 8', Ch. to Ped. 8'

BGK1084 Joy To The World Carolyn Hamlin Organ